Child's Guide to Stoicism: Life's Lessons for Young Minds

Andrés Correa U.

INDEX

Prologue

Hello, brave explorers of wisdom and seekers of life's mysteries! Are you ready for an amazing adventure that will take you on a journey like no other? If your answer is yes, then let's embark on this magical ride into the world of Stoic philosophy.

Yes, you heard it right, Stoicism! It may sound like a big word, but don't worry. It's just a fancy name for some pretty cool ideas about life that have been around for a long, long time.

We'll meet characters that could have stepped right out of your favorite stories. From brave lions to persistent penguins, wise owls to patient tortoises, each has a tale to share and a lesson to impart.

This isn't just a book, it's a guide—a guide to understanding life and how to navigate it with courage, wisdom, and inner peace. We'll explore exciting ideas, hear wonderful stories, and engage in fun activities that will help you understand and embrace these teachings in your own life.

But remember, this isn't a journey you have to make all at once. You can take your time. Visit each chapter at your own pace, because learning is not a race, but a journey to be enjoyed.

So, are you ready, adventurers? Let's open the door to a world of wisdom and step into the realm of Stoicism.

A wonderful, enlightening adventure awaits!

Now, turn the page and let's begin our journey with our first lesson. Are you ready? Let's go!

Chapter 1: Embracing Change

1.1 What is Change?

Change is an integral part of life and the world around us. It's the process through which something becomes different, either gradually or suddenly. You can see examples of change in everything from the seasons to your own growth. The leaves turn from green to gold in the autumn, and you are taller this year than you were last year. Those are both examples of change.

In the context of Stoicism, change is seen as a natural and inevitable part of life. Stoics believe in accepting and adapting to change rather than resisting it. They view change as an opportunity for growth and learning. They suggest that instead of fearing change, we should embrace it, understanding that it's a part of the natural flow of life.

1.2 The Story of the Unstoppable River

Once upon a time, there was a small, peaceful village nestled in the heart of a forest. The villagers relied on a river that flowed through their land for their water needs. This river was a symbol of constancy and continuity for the villagers. It had always been there, never changing its course or its flow.

One day, a powerful storm caused the river to swell and change its course, threatening to flood the village. The villagers panicked, trying to build barriers to stop the river, but it was too strong and kept changing its course.

In the midst of the panic, a wise old villager stood calmly, watching the river. He realized that instead of trying to stop the river, they should adapt to its new course. He rallied the villagers and suggested building their homes higher up the riverbank, where the water couldn't reach. The villagers followed his advice, and the village was saved.

The villagers learned an invaluable lesson that day about the power of change and the importance of adapting to it rather than trying to resist it. They realized that change is an integral part of life and can lead to growth and new opportunities if embraced positively.

1.3 Time Capsule

For this activity, you will need a small box or container, some paper and a pen, and any personal items you'd like to include. This time capsule will help you understand and appreciate the concept of change.

First, write a letter to your future self. You can include your current hobbies, favorite things, dreams, and how you see the world right now. Next, add a few personal items that represent you at this moment. It could be a favorite toy, a picture, or a piece of art you've created.

Then, bury your time capsule in

your backyard or hide it somewhere safe. Set a reminder for yourself to open it one year from now. When the time comes, you'll be surprised at how much you've changed in just a year. You'll have grown physically, emotionally, and mentally. You'll see that change isn't something to fear, but a natural part of life to embrace and learn from.

Chapter 2: The Power of Acceptance

2.1 Understanding Acceptance

Acceptance is the act of recognizing reality and embracing it as it is, without trying to deny or change it. It's a conscious choice to face the facts, to understand that some things are beyond our control, and to be at peace with that.

In the context of Stoicism, acceptance is a fundamental principle. Stoics emphasize accepting everything as it comes, without wishing for it to be different. They believe that our happiness and tranquility depend on our ability to accept life as it is rather than how we wish it to be. This doesn't mean we should be passive or indifferent, but that we should focus our efforts where we have control and accept what we don't.

2.2 The Tale of the Willow Tree

Once upon a time, there were two trees in the forest: an oak tree and a willow tree. They stood side by side, weathering the seasons together.

One day, a fierce storm swept through the forest. The strong winds battered against the trees, threatening to uproot them. The oak tree stood rigid, refusing to sway with the winds. It tried to resist the force of the storm, only to be eventually uprooted by the relentless winds.

On the other hand, the willow tree did not resist. It swayed with the winds, bending but not breaking. It accepted the power of the storm and moved with it rather than against it. When the storm passed, the willow tree was still standing, while the oak tree lay uprooted on the forest floor.

The story of the willow tree teaches us the power of acceptance. It shows us that by accepting and adapting to circumstances, we can survive and thrive, even in the face of adversity.

2.3 Acceptance Collage

For this activity, you'll need a blank sheet of paper, some magazines or newspapers, a pair of scissors, and glue.

The goal of this activity is to create a visual representation of acceptance.

Go through the magazines or newspapers and cut out images or words that represent acceptance to you. It could be a picture of a peaceful landscape, a quote about acceptance, or anything else that resonates with you.

Once you have your images and words, arrange them on your sheet of paper in a way that feels right to you. Glue them down to create your acceptance collage. When you're done, spend a few moments looking at your collage. Let it remind you of the power of acceptance and how it can bring peace and resilience into your life.

Chapter 3: Living in the Present

3.1 Exploring the Present Moment

The present moment, often referred to as 'now', is the time that we are currently living and experiencing. It's where life happens. The past has already occurred and can't be changed, while the future is yet to come and remains uncertain. The only time we truly have control over is the present.

In the philosophy of Stoicism, living in the present moment is a key principle. Stoics emphasize the importance of focusing on the 'now' and making the most of it, instead of dwelling on past regrets or future anxieties. They believe that true contentment and peace can be found by fully embracing and experiencing the present moment.

3.2 The Parable of the Forgetful Elephant

Once upon a time in the deep jungle, there lived an elephant named Elly. Elly was very forgetful. She was always thinking about the past and the future, which made her forget what she was doing in the present.

One day, Elly was walking by the river and saw a delicious fruit hanging from a tree. She reached out with her trunk to grab the fruit, but she started thinking about how she had failed to get the fruit the last time. As she was lost in her thoughts about the past, she didn't notice that a group of ants had started climbing her leg.

Next, she started worrying about whether she would be able to get the fruit next time. While she was caught up in her thoughts about the future, she didn't notice that the ants had reached her back.

Suddenly, she felt a tickling sensation and realized that she was covered in ants! She quickly shook them off and then refocused her attention on the fruit. This time, she didn't think about the past or the future. She just focused on the present moment and easily grabbed the fruit with her trunk.

Elly's story teaches us the importance of living in the present. When we are too focused on the past or the future, we might miss out on what's happening right now.

3.3 The Here and Now Treasure Hunt

This activity is designed to help children practice mindfulness and focus on the present moment. For this activity, you will need various objects or toys.

Hide these objects around your house or yard. The goal of the treasure hunt is not just to find the objects but to pay close attention to the surroundings during the hunt. Encourage the child to notice the colors, textures, sounds, and smells around them.

After the treasure hunt, ask them to

share what they noticed during the activity. This could include how an object felt in their hands, a sound they heard, or a smell they noticed. This activity not only makes mindfulness fun but also helps children develop a habit of living in the present moment.

Chapter 4: The Joy of Simplicity

4.1 The Beauty of Simplicity

Simplicity refers to the state or quality of being simple. It is about choosing less over more, clarity over complexity, and tranquility over chaos. Simplicity is not about deprivation or lack, but about removing the unnecessary and focusing on what truly matters.

In Stoicism, simplicity holds a significant place. Stoics view simplicity as a path to freedom and contentment. They believe that by reducing our desires and needs, and by focusing on the essentials, we can reduce stress and find true happiness. Simplicity, in Stoic philosophy, allows us to enjoy life's simple pleasures and to live in harmony with nature.

4.2 The Story of the Contented Sparrow

Once upon a time, there was a sparrow named Sammy. Unlike other birds who were always looking for bigger nests and more food, Sammy was content with his simple life.

Sammy had a small nest, but it was cozy and comfortable. He ate simple food, but it was fresh and tasty. Sammy didn't have many possessions, but he had everything he needed.

One day, a group of sparrows visited Sammy's nest. They were surprised by his simple living and couldn't understand why he didn't want more. They tried to convince Sammy to seek bigger nests, hoard more food, and collect shiny objects. But Sammy politely declined.

He said, "I have a warm nest, enough food, and peace of mind. What more do I need? More possessions would only bring more worries."

The visiting sparrows were confused, but Sammy was at peace. He continued to live his simple life and remained content and happy. Sammy's story teaches us that happiness is not found in possessions or complexity, but in simplicity and contentment.

4.3 Simple Pleasures Diary

For this activity, you'll need a notebook and a pen or pencil. This notebook will be your "Simple Pleasures Diary."

Every day for a week, take a few minutes to write down one simple pleasure that you enjoyed that day. It could be anything from a warm ray of sunshine on your face, the taste of a fresh apple, a hug from a friend, or the smell of fresh flowers.

At the end of the week, take some time to read through your diary. Reflect on the joy these simple pleasures brought you and how they enriched your life.

This activity helps to cultivate an

appreciation for life's simple pleasures and encourages the practice of living simply and mindfully.

Chapter 5: Self-Control and Willpower

5.1 Understanding Self-Control

Self-control, sometimes called self-discipline, is the ability to control our emotions, behaviors, and desires to achieve long-term goals. It's about being able to say "no" to immediate pleasures or distractions in favor of more significant gains in the future.

In the realm of Stoicism, self-control is of utmost importance. Stoics teach that we should strive to master our responses to the world around us, not be slaves to our desires. By practicing self-control, we can maintain a steady mind, make rational decisions, and live in harmony with our principles.

5.2 The Fable of the Patient Tortoise

In a quiet corner of the forest, lived a tortoise named Tilly. Tilly was known for her incredible self-control and patience.

One day, a hare challenged Tilly to a race, thinking that his speed would guarantee him a win. But Tilly accepted the challenge without hesitation. The other animals watched in anticipation as the race began.

The hare dashed off quickly, leaving Tilly behind. But Tilly didn't rush or try to match the hare's speed. Instead, she moved at her steady pace, maintaining her self-control.

Seeing Tilly far behind, the hare

decided to take a nap. He thought he could still win the race even if he rested for a while.

But while the hare slept, Tilly continued her slow and steady journey. She never wavered, kept her pace, and exercised incredible self-control.

By the time the hare woke up, Tilly was just a step away from the finish line. Despite his fast running, the hare couldn't catch up, and Tilly won the race. Tilly's self-control and patience paid off and taught everyone a valuable lesson that slow and steady (or self-controlled and patient) can indeed win the race.

5.3 The Willpower Challenge

For this activity, you'll need to choose a simple challenge that requires some level of self-control or willpower. It could be anything from not eating a favorite snack for a week, waking up earlier than usual, or spending less time watching TV or playing video games.

Track your progress throughout the week. Write down any difficulties you face, how you overcome them, and how you feel each day. At the end of the week, reflect on the experience. What did you learn about yourself? How did it feel to exercise self-control?

This activity aims to help children understand the concept of self-control better, recognize its value, and practice developing it in a fun and engaging way.

Chapter 6: Courage to Face Fear

6.1 Embracing Courage

Courage is the ability to face danger, fear, or changes without being overcome by anxiety or fear. It's the strength to stand up to anything that scares us and to step out of our comfort zone. Courage, in the Stoic philosophy, isn't just about being fearless. It's about acknowledging our fears and deciding to move forward regardless.

Stoics argue that courage is essential in life as it empowers us to confront all kinds of difficulties and challenges. It's not about the absence of fear, but about the decision to act despite the fear.

6.2 The Lion and the Mouse: A Stoic Tale

In the heart of the jungle, lived a fearsome lion named Leo. One day, a little mouse named Max accidentally disturbed Leo's sleep. Enraged, Leo was about to crush the tiny creature.

But Max, although trembling with fear, gathered all his courage and pleaded, "Please, King Leo, spare my life, and I promise to repay your kindness someday." Leo, amused by this promise, let the mouse go.

Days later, Leo was trapped by hunters. He roared and struggled but couldn't escape. Hearing the lion's roars, Max rushed to the scene. Without wasting a moment, Max started gnawing at the ropes with his sharp little teeth.

Despite his fear of the hunters, Max exhibited tremendous courage and managed to free Leo. In the end, it was the small and fearful mouse who saved the mighty lion's life. This story teaches us that no matter how small or scared we are, we can accomplish great things with courage.

6.3 The Courage Shield

For this activity, you'll need a piece of paper and some colors. Draw a large shield on the paper. This is your 'Courage Shield'.

Now, think about the things that you are scared of or make you uncomfortable. Write these things outside the shield.

Inside the shield, write down actions you can take to face these fears. They can be small steps to conquer your fears gradually.

Hang this shield somewhere you can see every day. Every time you face a fear and take action towards overcoming it, color that part of the shield.

This activity helps children identify their fears and encourages them to take steps towards overcoming them. It's a visual representation of their courage in the face of fear.

Chapter 7: Valuing Wisdom

7.1 What is Wisdom?

Wisdom is the ability to use knowledge and experience to make good decisions and judgments. It's more than just knowing facts or information. Wisdom involves understanding, insight, and the ability to apply knowledge to different situations in life. In Stoicism, wisdom is the most valuable virtue. Stoics believe that wisdom helps us distinguish between what is under our control and what is not, leading to peace and contentment.

7.2 The Wise Old Owl's Secret

In the depths of the green forest lived an old owl, renowned for his wisdom. Animals from near and far would come to seek his advice.

One day, a curious squirrel asked the owl, "Old Owl, what's your secret? How are you so wise?"

The owl responded, "The secret, young one, is to observe, listen, and think before you act. You learn when you observe others, gain knowledge when you listen, and gain wisdom when you think about applying what you've learned in your life."

The squirrel was astounded by the owl's wisdom, but then realized it wasn't a secret. The owl was wise because he constantly learned from his experiences and used that knowledge thoughtfully.

7.3 The Wisdom Seeker's Journal

For this activity, start a "Wisdom Seeker's Journal". Every day for a week, jot down something new you've learned. It could be a fact from a book, a life lesson from a movie, or something you observed.

Next to each entry, write down how you can apply this knowledge in your life. At the end of the week, reflect on the entries. You'll notice how much you've learned and how you've started to think wisely about applying what you've learned.

This activity helps children to

appreciate learning and wisdom. It encourages them to think about what they've learned and how they can apply that knowledge in their lives, fostering wisdom.

8: The Importance of Duty

8.1 Exploring Duty

Duty is a moral or legal obligation; a responsibility. It's something you should do because it's morally right or because the law requires it. Stoics placed great importance on fulfilling one's duties. They believed that each of us has a role to play in the grand scheme of the universe, and fulfilling our duties is how we play our part.

8.2 The Ant's Task: A Story of Responsibility

In a small crevice in the ground lived a diligent ant named Andy. Unlike other ants, Andy was often seen carrying twice his weight and working non-stop.

One day, a grasshopper asked Andy, "Why do you work so hard, Andy? Take a break and enjoy the sun like I do."

Andy replied, "I have a duty to collect food for the colony, and I take it very seriously. We all have a role to play, and we must fulfill our duties with commitment and determination."

Soon, the winter came, and the grasshopper found himself without any food or shelter. Meanwhile, Andy and his colony were safe and well-fed, thanks to their hard work and commitment to their duty. The grasshopper realized the importance of duty and how crucial it is to take responsibilities seriously.

8.3 The Duty Star

For this activity, draw a big star on a piece of paper. Write 'Duty Star' at the top. Think about five duties or responsibilities you have. It could be anything from feeding your pet, helping with chores, to doing homework. Write one duty on each point of the star.

Every day for the next week, make a mark next to each duty when you complete it. At the end of the week, look at your Duty Star. How does it feel to see all the duties you've fulfilled? This activity helps you understand the concept of duty and encourages you to take your responsibilities seriously.

Chapter 9: Inner Peace and Harmony

9.1 Discovering Inner Peace

Inner peace is a state of being mentally and spiritually at peace, with enough knowledge and understanding to keep oneself strong in the face of discord or stress. For Stoics, inner peace comes from understanding and accepting the world as it is, focusing on what's in our control, and letting go of the rest.

9.2 The Tale of the Peaceful Dolphin

In the deep blue sea, there lived a serene dolphin named Dolly. Unlike the other sea creatures who were often frantic, Dolly was always calm, moving smoothly through the water.

One day, a young fish, agitated by the chaos in the sea, asked Dolly, "Why are you always so calm amidst the frenzy?" Dolly smiled and replied, "I can only control my actions and my reactions. The sea can be peaceful or stormy, but I choose to swim through it with grace and tranquility."

From that day on, the young fish tried to be more like Dolly, focusing on what he could control, his actions and reactions, and found a sense of inner peace even amidst the chaos of the sea.

9.3 The Harmony Drawing

For this activity, find a quiet space

and take a few deep breaths to center yourself. Now, take a sheet of paper and some colors. Draw a picture that represents harmony to you. It could be a calm sea, a quiet forest, or anything else that you associate with peace and tranquility.

While drawing, focus on the calm and peace you feel. When you finish, write down how you felt while drawing and how you can bring that feeling of calm and peace into your daily life.

This activity not only stimulates creativity but also helps children understand the concept of inner peace and encourages them to find ways to cultivate it in their lives.

Chapter 10: The Power of Resilience

10.1 Understanding Resilience

Resilience is the ability to bounce back from adversity, disappointment, and failure. It's about being able to keep going in the face of challenges and not give up. The Stoics valued resilience and believed it was key to enduring life's ups and downs. By understanding that hardships are a part of life, we can develop resilience and navigate challenges with greater ease.

10.2 The Story of the Persistent Penguin

In the icy lands of Antarctica, there lived a small but persistent penguin named Pip. Pip was smaller than most penguins, and he often struggled to keep up with the rest.

One day, a harsh storm blew away all the food and Pip was left without anything to eat. Despite the circumstances, Pip didn't lose hope. He journeyed through snow and wind, climbing icebergs and swimming in freezing waters, determined to find food. His persistence paid off, and he managed to find a small school of fish.

The other penguins were amazed at Pip's resilience. Despite being smaller and faced with the same difficult circumstances, Pip didn't give up. He showed them all the power of resilience.

10.3 The Resilience Rock

For this activity, find a rock. This is your Resilience Rock. Decorate it in any way you like. Once decorated, place your Resilience Rock somewhere you can see it every day.

Whenever you face a challenge or setback, hold the rock and remember Pip the Penguin. Remember how he didn't give up, no matter how hard things got. Think about how you can be resilient like Pip.

This activity serves as a tangible reminder of resilience, helping children to cultivate this valuable trait in their own lives.

Epilogue

Wow, brave adventurers, you've made it! You've journeyed through the chapters of Stoicism, unraveling wisdom, courage, simplicity, and resilience along the way. You've learned, you've reflected, and you've grown. But remember, this is not the end of your journey.

Stoicism is a lifelong adventure, a constant journey of learning, growing, and understanding. The tales you've heard and the activities you've undertaken, they are just the beginning. As you continue to grow, so will your understanding of these lessons. And remember, just like Pip the Penguin, no matter how challenging life may get, you have the strength to keep going.

You are now carriers of ancient wisdom, explorers of life's mysteries, and seekers of truth. Remember to revisit these lessons from time to time, apply them to your daily life, and share your knowledge with others.

Embrace the beauty of change like the Unstoppable River. Live in the present moment like the Forgetful Elephant. Find joy in simplicity like the Contented Sparrow, and always have the courage to face fear like the Lion and the Mouse. Value wisdom like the Wise Owl, understand the importance of duty like the Responsible Ant, and find your inner peace like the Peaceful Dolphin. And, of course, never forget the power of resilience shown by the

Persistent Penguin.

We are incredibly proud of the journey you've embarked on by reading this book, and we can't wait to see how you use these lessons in your life. The world is your book of wisdom, and every moment is a page waiting to be read.

Remember, brave adventurers, the journey doesn't end here. Keep exploring, keep asking questions, and most importantly, keep learning. After all, life is the most exciting adventure of all! Until our next journey together, farewell!

32284351R00040